Grieve With Guidance

a 30-day guide to support you on your journey through loss and forgiveness

CHRISTINE MARIE

Copyright © 2025 by Christine Marie. All rights reserved.

No part of this book may be reproduced, stored in a retrieval system, or transmitted in any form or by any means—electronic, mechanical, photocopying, recording, or otherwise—without the prior written permission of the publisher, except in the case of brief quotations embodied in critical reviews and certain other noncommercial uses permitted by copyright law.

Published by Christine Marie

ISBN: 979-8-35099-341-7

The information provided is for educational and inspirational purposes only and is not intended as a substitute for professional advice. The author and publisher assume no responsibility for any actions taken based on the content of this book.

For permissions or inquiries, contact:
Christine Marie
www.christinemarieheals.com

Printed in the United States of America
First Edition: 2025

Dedication

This book is dedicated to my father, Gary Martin Aitchison who left this life on March 12th, 2024.

Thank you for being what inspired me to create this offering with unconditional love and forgiveness. Thank you for your teachings, Dad. I love you.

To grieve deeply is to know love in its purest form.

Leaning into our personal grief is a sacred act—one that often requires courage, surrender and the cultivation of trust in the Great Mystery.

Once we begin to understand the non-linear nature of grief after we lose someone we love, we open our hearts to receive greater access to self-compassion, peace and acceptance. To lean toward the ache is a true gift—but uncovering it calls us to walk a path that isn't easy.

I am here to give you full permission to experience your grief in all its complexity and encourage your heart to expand into more truth, vulnerability, and divinity than before your loss.

Practicing self-care, engaging in rituals of remembrance, and finding meaning in the midst of loss can all be helpful strategies for navigating the waves of grief.
.
It is an honor and privilege to support you in your grieving process. May this offering assure you that you are not alone. I am here, holding you every step of the way.

Your Guidebook Includes:
Rituals
Journal Prompts
Bonus Offerings
Guided Meditations
Specialized Grieve with Guidance Playlist

What You Will Need:
Candle
Rose Tea
Sacred Space
This Guidebook
Curated Grieve with Guidance Playlist

How to use this Guidebook

Make sure you create a quiet, sacred space where you aren't interrupted throughout your daily practice. Once you begin, press play on the Grieve With Guidance playlist. *Note that you can spend about 5-25 minutes on each exercise.*

Access Playlist: christinemarieheals.com/grievewithguidance

It's not crucial to go in order, however, I do recommend doing so for your first time. If one practice doesn't resonate or doesn't seem doable, feel free to skip & come back to it when you're ready.

I suggest brewing your cup of Rose tea and sipping it every morning prior to your guided practice. Rose is a wonderful plant spirit that helps in releasing grief, connecting to our creative center, & provides us with the energetic protection and strength to move forward with our emotions risen at the surface.

Take really good care of your mind, body and heart throughout this process. Take breaks. Drink water. Go for a walk after you've completed an exercise. Let yourself fully feel free to express your truth here. You can't do it wrong. You are fully supported and held with love and tenderness.

Contents

1... Acknowledging Grief & Cultivating Self-Compassion

14... Exploring Emotions & Finding Joy

25... Nurturing & Nourishing Your Body

38... Signs From Our Loved Ones, Embracing Change & Karmic Contracts

Day 1 - Journal Prompt:

Take some time to reflect on the loss you're grieving. Write about how it has impacted your life, what you miss most about who you lost, or even things you won't miss. Allow yourself to be fully honest here with your emotions without self-judgment. Anger, sadness, confusion, relief, guilt and denial are all valid and normal. *Note: No feeling is bad, wrong or too much.*

Notes:

Day 2 – Memory Candle Ritual:

Light a candle in remembrance of your loss. Spend a few moments in quiet reflection, gazing upon the flickering flame, allowing yourself to acknowledge the reality of your grief.

As you gaze into the flame, notice what's arising within your body and heart, and allow yourself the time and space to be with what's present.

This candle now represents the energy of who you lost. Make a point to come back to it throughout your grieving process in honor and remembrance. Write down anything that came through.

Day 3 - Self-Care Ritual:

Choose a date on the calendar and mark it off from any responsibilities or obligations. This day is where you can pause the world just for a moment and is dedicated towards you and your grief. Book a massage. Drive to the coast. Wander around your neighborhood. Stay in bed and binge-watch sad rom-coms. The world doesn't stop whenever we lose someone. Make this day count. This day is all about YOU!

Date:

Time:

Location:

Activity:

The Only Way

I hate to say that I'm relieved
and yet, when dawn meets day, the lilies pop,
the church bells sing—brighter
than the day
his heart beat like a flat drum on a winters night
his breath whispered songs as shallow
as the full moon tide

On these earthly planes
he knew not of peace

A free spirit at heart, he knew
death
was the only way

Acknowledging Grief & Cultivating Self-Compassion

Days 4-7

Fostering Self-Compassion

Day 4 - Journal Prompt:

Reflect on any self-critical thoughts or judgments you've been holding onto since your loss. Get curious around what's at the root behind these feelings. Where do they come from? Are they ancestral? Societal? How can you choose more acts of loving-kindness towards yourself?

_____
_____
_____
_____
_____
_____
_____
_____
_____
_____
_____
_____
_____

Notes:

Day 5 – Letter of Compassion Ritual:

Write a compassionate letter to yourself, acknowledging any internal pain and offering words of kindness and understanding.
Note: Treat yourself the way you would a Beloved friend.

Day 6 – Energy Cleansing Ritual:

Take a soothing bath or shower, imagining the warm water washing away any feelings of guilt or self-blame. Repeat affirmations of self-love, forgiveness & acceptance until you feel a clearing:

"It is okay to take time away to be with myself and my emotions. It is not selfish to take care of myself."

"I forgive myself for any mistakes or shortcomings. I am human and deserve forgiveness."

"I release any resentment or anger towards myself. I choose to embrace peace and acceptance."

"I am free from the burden of guilt and shame. I forgive myself and allow in grace."

"I trust in my ability to heal and grow within this loss. It is okay to be patient with the process."

"I am worthy of love and compassion, exactly as I am."

Day 7 – Guided Meditation:

Guided Meditation with Mother Earth

Feeling overwhelmed by your emotions? Allow yourself to connect with the natural world's inherent healing power. This meditation will guide you through grounding techniques and imagery to find comfort and release in the embrace of Mother Earth.

Visit here: christinemarieheals.com/grievewithguidance

Once you have finished your guided meditation, feel free to write down any thoughts, feelings or emotions that show up.

River of Tears

Your grief is the gateway to forgiveness
The rivers you cry do not make you weak;
they grant you the gift of release

Your tears set you free

Exploring Emotions and Finding Joy

Days 8-10

Creatively Exploring & Expressing Feelings

Day 8 – Explore the Mystery Ritual:

Take some time to explore your emotions through creative self-expression. Write a poem or draw a picture below, that expresses the truth of your emotions. *Remember to leave behind perfectionism here and just have fun exploring your inner landscape.*

Day 9 – Artist Date Collage Ritual:

Set aside one-hour of dedicated time for expression through collaging. Gather some magazines and scissors, and then pick an inspiring corner of your home or a favorite local coffee shop. As you flip through the pages, cut out anything that feels connected to your inner world of grief. Let your emotions guide your art. Once you've finished, write down below words to describe your collage to seal in your ritual.

Day 10 – Asking for Support Ritual:

Write down at least one-to-three people who you can trust and have shown up for you during your grieving process. Mark a day on your calendar to reach out to them and see if they are available for holding space for you while you process your emotions. Let yourself lean into receiving love and support and simply notice if anything has shifted energetically in your body after you've done this practice.

Name

Date

Name

Date

Name

Date

Follow Me Home

*I know
I cannot save you
I know
I have no control
over the way your story ends*

*But my hands are here,
reaching out for you
Hoping that somehow,
someday,
yours will grasp them
and follow me home*

Exploring Emotions & Finding Joy

Days 11-14

Experiencing Joy & Love

Day 11 - Journal Prompt:

Spend time looking through old photos, letters, or mementos that remind you of your loved one. Write about a happy memory you shared together and reflect on the joy it brings you.

Notes:

Day 12 - Memory Altar Ritual:

Create a memory altar featuring items that represent your loved one and the special moments you shared. Spend time adding to it each day as you uncover more memories. Create a sacred space where this altar resides so you can always return to it whenever you desire closeness & connection.

Memory Altar Items:

1.
2.
3.
4.
5.
6.
7.

Day 13 - Memory Candle Ritual:

Grab your memory candle from the first week and add it to your altar. Take another few moments to light and gaze at the candle, beginning to share aloud any feelings or messages you'd like this person to receive. Maybe it's just as simple as sending them love energetically from your heart space.

Remember Me - For Everett Young

When dawn comes, let yourself be still,
for I am with you—
within the rays of sun
and the light of the moon

When your heart feels heavy,
must you always remember
the way my smile lit up the room
every moment I was with you

When you miss me most
do not ever fear
my Spirit lives within the sun
I will dry away your tears

When the clouds come rolling in
listen to these words
for the love we share is stronger than most,
our bond can never be broken

When you cannot sleep, must you think of me
Though my body may be gone,
my soul lives to carry on,
your sole protector, I will always be

Nurturing & Nourishing Your Body

Days 15-17

Your Body is a Temple

Day 15 – Journal Prompt:

Dear body, what would you have me know about my grief today?

Notes:

Day 16 - Movement is Medicine Ritual:

Pay attention to your body's needs today. Place one hand on your heart and one hand on your belly. Tune in and choose a physical activity from the list below that feels nourishing.

- [ ] Yoga
- [ ] Pilates
- [ ] Dancing
- [ ] Qigong
- [ ] Bike Ride
- [ ] Gentle Walk
- [ ] Weight Lifting
- [ ] Forest Bathing
- [ ] Light Stretching
- [ ] Other

Day 17 – Journal Prompt:

Note down what came up for you physically, emotionally, and/or spiritually when you practiced your movement exercise. How did you feel before and after you moved your body in this way?

Notes:

May Peace Be With You

*Somedays,
i wish his body to leave this earth
just so his mind could be at peace*

Nurturing & Nourishing Your Body

Days 18-20

Medicine from the Earth

Day 18 – Food is Medicine Reflection:

How has your relationship to food been like since the loss? Has it been balanced with nutritional, life-giving meals? Without judgment, reflect on what kind of nutrition has been supportive. How can you support yourself more moving forward?

Day 19 – Rose Ritual & Recipe:

In times of devasting loss, gentle care & self-compassion are a must. Show up for yourself with this warming *Self-Love Rose Beet Latte.* Loaded with heart protecting vitamins, stress reducing adaptogens, brain boosting minerals, & anti-inflammatory ingredients. It's easy to make and nurturing for the soul. Sip, heal, & be in bliss.

Prep time: 5 min
Ritual Time: 10-15 min
Yield: 1 Serving

Ingredients:
1/2 teaspoon rose petal powder
1/2 teaspoon Maca
1/2 teaspoon beet powder
1-2 teaspoon maple syrup
1 teaspoon collagen powder
¼ teaspoon vanilla extract or vanilla paste
1 cup of oat milk (or your favorite plant-based milk)
1 cup water

Self-Love Rose Beet Latte Recipe:

Instructions:
1. Boil the hot water.
2. Grab your favorite oversized cozy mug.
3. Combine the rose petal powder, beet powder, vanilla, and maple syrup together with 1 cup boiled filtered water.
4. Use a blender or frothier and mix until smooth, then pour into your mug.
5. Pour the plant-based milk.
6. Top with editable flowers, cinnamon or cardamom rose dust (optional).

Ritual:
Sip your latte while nourishing your heart chakra. Hold a rose quartz crystal up to your heart and repeat the affirmation:

"I am gentle with myself as I heal. This pain will ease in time."

By Shannon Kaiser, Author of *The Self-Love Experiment*
https://radicalbodylovewithshannon.com/

Day 20 - Rose Reflection:

Rose is a powerful plant that helps support the movement of grief throughout the physical and energetic bodies. Her spirit is connected to the Divine Feminine, and is one of the most high vibrational plants there are.

Write about what it was like to connect with the energy of Rose. How did it taste? What guidance, messages, healings or teachings is Rose giving you?

Dear Great Mother

This morning, I choose
to focus my energy
on what is here
instead of what is missing

Like the first drops of morning rain
singing on the roof,
Or the taste of fresh plantains
greeting my mouth when I wake
Or the endless hours of being at rest,
while the world crosses tasks off
its to-do list

This morning I choose ecstasy
in the present-day slowness
bow to the here and now,
and rinse off yesterday's mishaps

This morning, I choose
to breathe forgiveness deep-
exhaling shame, I set my burdens free
down to Mother Earth
with my barren knees

Dearest Great Mother, take all of what is not mine to carry-
the lost parts and misaligned frequencies
no longer mine to keep

This morning I choose to welcome gratitude
for the womb that holds and rebirths me

Signs From Our Loved Ones, Embracing Change & Karmic Contracts

Days 21-24

You Are Not Alone

Day 21 - Guided Meditation:
Connection to a Loved One

This guided meditation provides a safe space for you to connect with your loved one in spirit. I'll guide you through a visualization exercise to find solace, while strengthening the bond you share, even in their physical absence.

Visit here: christinemarieheals.com/grievewithguidance

Once you have finished your guided meditation, feel free to write down any thoughts, feelings or emotions that show up.

Day 22 - Watching for Signs Ritual:

Plan to take a long walk in nature and state the intention for a sign from the spirit of your loved one to come through.

On your walk, pay attention to all of your senses and notice what you see, smell, taste or hear and be still in silence with curiosity. Keep this question alive like a flame in your heart, allowing yourself to receive any messages or insights that are here for you.

*Note that animals and humans can embody a guide or guardian angel in this third-dimensional reality, be open to that possibility and take notice if you come across a stranger out of the blue with a sign for you.

Day 23 - Dream Ritual:

Place this page open next to your bed tonight. Say to yourself right before you fall asleep, "Dear ____ (name of who has passed) show me a sign to connect with you in my dreams tonight."

Write down anything and everything you can remember from your dream right when you wake (or even in the middle of the night) for more signs and guidance.

_____
_____
_____
_____
_____
_____
_____
_____
_____
_____
_____

Notes:

Day 24 – Spiritual Connection Reflection:

Explore your spiritual beliefs and how they have been affected by your loss. Write about any moments of connection or transcendence you've experienced during your grieving process.

Did anything surprise you? Did you see or notice any synchronicities, messages or signs from the other side?

*Note that nothing is too "abnormal" here, trust your intuition.

Notes:

Know Love, Know Grief

What agony it is,
to be swallowed up by oceans of grief

What beauty it is,
to know this kind of love

Signs From Our Loved Ones, Embracing Change & Karmic Contracts

Days 25-28

Embracing Change

Day 25 - Death & Rebirth Reflection:

Despite your pain, try to cultivate a sense of hope for the future. Reflect on the ways your life has changed since your loss. What has been released energetically, physically or emotionally?

Reflection: Death in any form is often a sign of change and rebirth. Write about any new opportunities or insights that have emerged from this grief journey. *Note it's more than okay to hold both sadness and joy at the same time. This is your permission slip to be human and experience the full spectrum of emotions.*

Notes:

Day 26 – Planting New Seeds Ritual:

Take a symbolic action to mark the transition into a new phase of your life-whether it's planting a tree, beginning a new creative project, or learning a new skill that supports your rebirthing process. What does your heart and soul yearn to create or manifest? Dream big here.

Day 27 - Moving Forward Ritual:

Below, free write using simple words to describe the energy behind your future endeavors. Then, create a vision board featuring images that represent this energy. Spend time visualizing these dreams coming to fruition and holding onto them as beacons of light in dark times. Place it on your altar alongside your other sacred objects to bring about hope and balance.

If Loneliness Had a Name

*If loneliness had a name,
it would be one I could always remember
If it had a sound,
it would echo through the night
while shadows dance in emptiness*

*When all is dark and abandoned,
loneliness would wear the arms of winter,
cradled within my longing*

*For warmth,
I reach
until my arms grow tired*

*For love,
I weep
until my heart stops beating*

Signs From Our Loved Ones, Embracing Change & Karmic Contracts

Days 28-30

Forgiveness & Karmic Contracts

Day 28 - Dear Loved One Ritual:

When we lose someone we love, it's normal to experience a range of emotions from sorrow, rage, and even relief. Reflect on any feelings of anger or resentment you may be holding onto. Write a letter of forgiveness to yourself or the other you've lost, releasing any lingering negative emotions still present within. Remember, forgiveness is a process.

Dear _____(name),

_____
_____
_____
_____
_____
_____
_____
_____
_____
_____
_____
_____

Notes:

Day 29 - Karmic Lessons Ritual:

Every person who is a part of our life is here to teach us something profound about ourselves and the human experience. Reflect on some of the lessons this person taught you, understanding the karmic contract your souls agreed upon to learn from another. At the end, thank them for their teachings.

Day 30 - Forgiveness Ritual:

Practice a forgiveness meditation, visualizing yourself and the other being free from the burden of past hurts. Offer words of compassion and forgiveness to yourself and to the other.

The Ho'oponopono prayer is a Hawaiian forgiveness practice that involves repeating four simple phrases. The prayer is used to release negative emotions, heal relationships, and bring about inner peace.

The idea behind the Ho'oponopono prayer is that by sincerely repeating these phrases, you take responsibility for any negative energy or conflicts, ask for forgiveness, express gratitude, and affirm love.

When using the Ho'oponopono prayer, it's essential to say the phrases out loud with sincerity and an open heart. Whether you're seeking forgiveness for yourself, expressing gratitude, or sending love to others, the intention behind the words is crucial.

Utilize the ho'oponopono prayer to seal in the practice:

"I'm sorry."
"Please forgive me."
"Thank you."
"I love you."

Forgiveness

*You learned to love me
to the best of your ability.*

*I learned to forgive you
for your humanness.*

Concluding thoughts...

You have now entered a new threshold of personal healing—one of experiencing grief in all its complexity, challenge and beauty.

Take time to let this process marinate and unfold. Like every healing journey, grief follows a spiraled path—one that takes complete surrender and trust towards the Great Mystery.

Know that if you picked up this book, you are not behind. You are right on time.

I sincerely hope you now see life and death in a new light—that your heart feels a little lighter and your spirit ignited with new possibility.

Thank you for allowing me to earn your trust.

With love,
Christine Marie

Additional Resources

Looking for additional guidance on your grieving process?

Please feel free to reach out to Christine Marie directly if you'd like to schedule a grief healing session

Website: christinemarieheals.com
Substack: christinemarieheals.substack.com
IG: @christinemarieheals

About the Author

Christine Marie is a Medicine Woman who holds safe and sacred spaces for healing and transformation. She is a multi-faceted healer, spiritual mentor, writer and artist, weaving practices and teachings from indigenous peoples while pilgrimaging to Europe, Asia, Central, and South America where she has sat with world renowned shamans, spiritual teachers, and leaders who have re-awakened her connection towards her innate healing gifts.

She specializes in working with sacred plant medicines, energy healing, and creative self-expression ceremonies and practices.

She is the author of *Breaking Free*, winner of the Central Avenue Poetry Prize, and has been nominated for the Wordlights Poetry Showcase and continues to be an empowering voice for those who have survived trauma and abuse.